This Is No Time For Wimps!

by Charles R. Swindoll

D1713142

ZondervanPublishingHouse
Grand Rapids, Michigan

A Division of HarperCollins*Publishers*

This Is No Time for Wimps!

Copyright © 1994 by Charles R. Swindoll, Inc.

Requests for information should be addressed to:

Zondervan Publishing House
5300 Patterson Avenue S.E.
Grand Rapids, Michigan 49530

ISBN 0-310-48831-1

■   Printed in the United States of America

■   Cover Design by: DesignTeam, Brian L. Fowler

94 95 96 97 98 / ❖ LP / 5 4 3 2 1

This Is No Time
W^{FOR}imps!

Fifty years ago America was engaged in a struggle for survival.

We were sandwiched between two massive military powers bent on world domination. Our fighting forces were at their peak, performing at heroic levels of determination. Every magazine, every newspaper, every radio news report (there was no television), and virtually every conversation between neighbors and fellow employees included words about the war. It was, except for the bloody Civil War, the most significant war in our nation's history. Such a conflict called for stouthearted leaders who were not afraid . . . who could see the big picture . . . who were able to make tough and lonely decisions as well as motivate others who were willing to carry them out to the point of sacrifice.

Happily, Americans were not alone during those difficult and demanding years. Across the Atlantic the people of the United Kingdom remained staunch allies. A major part of the reason they stood with us so firmly was the courageous commitment of England's prime minister, a man whose leadership was nothing short of remarkable.

William Manchester refers to that man in his excellent volume *The Last Lion— Winston Spencer Churchill.*

> Like Adolf Hitler he would have to be a leader of intuitive genius, a born demagogue in the original sense of the word, a believer in the supremacy of his race and his national destiny, an artist who knew how to gather the blazing light of history into his prism and then distort it to his ends, an embodiment of inflexible resolution who could impose his will and imagination on his people— a great tragedian who understood the appeal of martyrdom and could tell his followers the worst, hurling it to them like great hunks of bleeding meat, persuading them that the year of Dunkirk would be one in which it was "equally good to live or to die"—who could if necessary be just as cruel, just as cunning, and just as ruthless as Hitler but who could win victories without enslaving populations, or preaching supernaturalism, or foisting off myths of his infallibility, or destroying, or even warping, the libertarian institutions he had

sworn to preserve. Such a man, if he existed, would be England's last chance.

In London there was such a man.[1]

STRONG WORDS FROM THE PAST

I can still remember listening to Churchill's moving and eloquent speeches that were often broadcast over radio. Though I was a lad of less than ten years of age, his words touched me deeply. I recall how often our family gathered around the radio, much like folks do in front of a televised broadcast today. I can also remember how my father would comment on the zeal and the determined fervor in the leader's words.

Recently, I decided it would be worth hearing again those immortal and timeless speeches. A friend loaned me several cassette tape recordings of Churchill's greatest speeches during those dark days when the Nazi *Luftwaffe* was conducting its merciless bombing raids on Great Britain. As I listened to the prime minister and tried to imagine the things he and his people were having to endure, I appreciated all the more his relentless determination. Backing away or surrendering were thoughts that never crossed his mind. Endurance, sacrifice, the discipline of durability—these were the things that characterized the man throughout the time he challenged his people to remain resolute.

Let me repeat excerpts from several of

Sir Winston Churchill's immortal speeches. Take your time as you read them. Keep in mind the historical context in which they were delivered. Try to imagine being there and enduring the devastation of bombing attacks and the threat of enemy invasion.

In his first address to the House of Commons on May 13, 1940, he said, "I have nothing to offer but blood, toil, tears, and sweat."[2] And again on June 4, 1940:

> Even though large tracts of Europe and many old and famous States have fallen or may fall into the grip of the Gestapo and all the odious apparatus of Nazi rule, we shall not flag or fail. We shall go on to the end, we shall fight in France, we shall fight on the seas and oceans, we shall fight with growing confidence and growing strength in the air, we shall defend our island, whatever the cost may be; we shall fight on the beaches, we shall fight on the landing grounds, we shall fight in the fields and in the streets, we shall fight in the hills; we shall never surrender. . . .[3] (Or, as he put it, "We shall *nevah surrendah!*")

In a speech to the London County Council a year later, July 14, 1941, he referred to "a comradeship of suffering and endurance."[4] A fresh surge of optimism overcame me when I heard those words. How strange they seemed in my ears—how rare they are today, fifty years later. He referred to Hitler and his Nazi horde: "We will have no truce or parley with you, or the grisly gang who work your wicked will. You do your worst—and we will do our best!"[5] Aren't those gallant words? (I like the way he referred to Hitler's "grisly gang.")

On October 29, 1941, he urged on the boys of Harrow School with these courageous words:

> Do not speak of darker days; let us speak rather of sterner days. These are not dark days; these are great days—the greatest days our country has ever lived; and we shall all thank God that we have been allowed, each one of us according to our stations, to play a part in making these days memorable in the history of our race.[6]

I especially like a part of the speech he delivered on December 30, 1941, in Ottawa, Canada, to the Canadian Senate and House of Commons:

> When I warned them [the French] that Britain would fight on alone whatever they did, their generals told their prime minister and his divided Cabinet, "In three weeks England will have her neck wrung like a chicken." Some chicken; some neck.[7]

What invincible courage! He was a man who could not tolerate the thought of giving up.

Let me return to another excerpt, this one delivered in the House of Commons, September 28. "Not in vain may be the pride of those who survived and the epitaph of those who fell."[8] What an enviable epitaph—"not in vain."

As I listened to him say those three words in his stately British accent, the thought flashed through my mind that he selected them, not from the back of his own brain, but from the passion of the apostle Paul in the New Testament. Can you remember when Paul used "not in vain"? He recorded them in his first letter to the Corinthians:

> Therefore, my beloved brethren, be steadfast, immovable, always abounding in the work of the Lord, knowing that in the Lord your labor is *not in vain*. [italics mine] (1 Cor. 15:58)

Churchill may have been eloquent and determined . . . but in that case, he was not original. Paul used those three words first. He didn't write them to the inhabitants of the British Isles, but to people living under the horrendous and horrible leadership of the Roman Caesar. They were hard times. They were harsh times. Not unlike what our nation experienced fifty years ago, back when I was a child. The good news is this: Hard times and harsh times spawn strong men and pioneer women—people who think straight, who refuse to surrender to wrong, who stand tall. People who do not bend and bow, who are willing to swim upstream rather than float aimlessly downriver with the current of public opinion. Such individuals, according to the Apostle of Grace, live lives "not in vain." "Nothing you do for the Lord is ever wasted," says *The Living Bible*.

It is the spirit of our roots that I want to emphasize in this booklet . . . the spirit of our country some fifty years ago; more importantly, the spirit from the passion of Paul.

HARD TIMES ARE HERE AGAIN

Hard days are not over; harsh times have not run their course. Quite frankly, we find ourselves in the midst of some of our greatest tests at this very moment. I am fully convinced we must again march in lockstep with the apostle. It will call for renewed determination, a commitment to faithfulness, and the constancy to endure. I would add that we must do so without reservation and without hesitation. Why? Because (again in the words of Churchill at the London County Council, July 14, 1941) of the "hideous, unprecedented, novel pressure"[9] of our times. It is time for us as a band of believers to recommit ourselves with steadfast determination to be people committed fully to the claims of Jesus Christ and to His cause. We must not . . . will not cave in. We will not capitulate. We will not weaken our stand. In fact, we will stand more firmly than ever. This is no time for wimps!

"Not failure, but low aim, is crime," wrote James Russell Lowell.[10] It was the same Lowell who wrote:

> Truth forever on the scaffold,
> Wrong forever on the throne;
> Yet that scaffold sways the future,
> And behind the dim unknown
> Standeth God within the shadows,
> Keeping watch above His own.[11]

There was once "such a man" in London who was not afraid to think differently ... who deliberately refused to allow hardship to discourage him. Are you "such a one" today? Perhaps you are one who is engaged in the gospel ministry. If so, great! You, of all people, must model strength of character. This is not a time to back away and surrender! John Henry Jowett said, "Ministry that costs nothing, accomplishes nothing."[12]

I thought of the dialogue I had the other day when a young, would-be Dallas Seminary student walked up alongside me, and said with a sigh, "You know, I'm really not sure I want to go to Dallas Seminary."

"Oh, really? Why not?" I asked. (I must confess that I was thinking, *Why wouldn't anybody training for ministry want to go to Dallas Seminary?*)

He answered, "Well, I've looked into the curriculum and found that it's so hard."

I said, "Isn't that great?"

He frowned and responded, "Well, that wasn't the adjective I had in mind when I said that."

I suggested, "Young man, it is the difficulty of it that gives you something to look back on with delight. Great character emerges out of tough times."

A CLOSER LOOK AT CHARACTER

May I repeat an earlier comment? It's the tough times that spawn greatness, or, to use the word that Churchill often used, "character . . . *charactah!*" The times in which we find ourselves call for strong character.

Dwight L. Moody once defined it: "Character is what you are in the dark."[13] The German poet, Johann Goethe, expressed it this way: "A talent is formed in stillness; character in the world's torrent."[14] True character usually has roots that go back to one's childhood. Thomas Paine was right: "Character is much easier kept than recovered."[15]

It's character that we are about, Christian brothers and sisters. It's greatness of character. You say, "Well, the times are hard and my days are tough to endure. In fact, I've been suffering a lot." Without trying to make light of the difficulties you are having to endure, let me welcome you to the club. You may not hear this from others, but I'm convinced that that is what the Christian life is all about. But I am certainly not among the first to point this out. For years, a few (always in the minority) have been telling the truth.

It was Aleksandr Solzhenitsyn, long before he was as well-known as he is today, who wrote in *The Gulag Archipelago*:

> It was only when I lay there on rotting prison straw that I sensed within myself the first stirrings of good. Gradually, it was disclosed to me that the line separating good and evil passes, not through states, nor between classes, nor between political parties either, but right through every human heart, and through all human hearts. So, bless you, prison, for having been in my life.[16]

(I can hardly quote those words without tears—tears of gratitude for such insight that comes from sacrifice.)

To borrow from that Russian statesman: Bless you, hardship, for having been in our childhood. Bless you, hard times, for giving us what we needed most. I am convinced that enduring hard times is one of the reasons today we admire great men and women. Hard times? Of course! They have come, which causes me to repeat, this is no time for wimps! Such times force you and me to take a fresh look at what drives us on

. . . and how we plan to invest our lives until Christ returns.

RETOOLING, NOT RETIRING!

The whole concept of retirement is not biblical; it's American. Before disagreeing, stop and think about it. Perhaps more than ever in our history, people in the workplace are literally living for the day when they can kick back, check out of reality, hang a "Do Not Disturb" sign on their door, and become disengaged from all responsibility. "After all," they say, "I've paid my dues." (I've never found that kind of thinking in the Scriptures!)

I had to face the facts some time ago that God was prompting a major move in my life. He was bringing about a change . . . an enormous "paradigm shift" in Chuck Swindoll's life. I had a wonderful situation in the church I'd served for almost twenty-three years. I mean, if you will allow me such an expression, I had it made. But I realized in the midst of it all that God hadn't said anything in His Word about "having it made." (I looked all the way through to find a little biblical support for having it made, taking it easy, relaxing, sitting in a rocking chair, watching hummingbirds suck red juice out of a jar, but I couldn't find anything!) But that's not what His Word talks about.

In fact, I find the very reason the apostle

Paul would say that we are to "be steadfast, immovable, abounding in the work" is because we do not have it made. We're not supposed to! God's plan is that we retool . . . not retire. Times are hard. Teach that to your children. Take your little grandchildren into your arms and whisper in their ears that life is difficult, that times are hard, and that's the way God has planned it on Planet Earth. Because without tough times, there would not be the cultivation of character. We'd all become a bunch of wimps!

A CLOSER LOOK AT CHARACTER

What is character? I keep referring to it, so perhaps I should define it. Character is, in my opinion, the moral, ethical, and spiritual undergirding that rests on truth, that reinforces a life in stressful times and resists all temptations to compromise. (Read that again, only this time, more slowly.) Next to salvation itself, I believe character is our greatest need and greatest safeguard.

While grazing through the rich and rewarding words of Hebrews 11 recently, it dawned on me that those in God's Hall of Faith were such people. Tucked away here in this ancient Westminster Abbey of Scripture, we find, listed by name, sixteen men and women of character. (If we include Joshua—see verses 29 and 30—we find no less than seventeen men and women listed in this grand Reader's Digest of the Old

Testament.) Actually, what we have here is a listing of people who not only thought straight and lived strongly . . . but finished well. What tough-minded people! Not perfect, understand . . . not a bunch of plaster saints, but not a wimp in the group. Each one, at some major point in life, had greatness of character. The names read like an all-time list of God's best. Names like Abel and Enoch and Noah and Abraham and Sarah and Isaac and Jacob and Joseph and Moses and Joshua and Rahab, et al. One remarkable person after another, including one remarkable act of faith after another. The writer seems to sum it all up when he asks:

> And what more shall I say? For time will fail me if I tell of Gideon, Barak, Samson, Jephthah, of David and Samuel and the prophets, who by faith conquered kingdoms, performed acts of righteousness, obtained promises, shut the mouths of lions, quenched the power of fire, escaped the edge of the sword, from weakness were made strong. (Heb. 11:32–34)

What were their times like? It's clear . . . they were hard, they were harsh . . . difficult beyond imagination. Some of those great saints were tortured. Others were sawn in two. The writer says they were stoned, tempted, wandering in sheepskins and goatskins, destitute, afflicted, tormented. What depressing scenes! Yet, those were people "of whom the world was not worthy." I find that statement one of the most eloquent in all the Bible. Such hard times spawned incredible people—the kind, we might say, who were too good for this old sin-cursed earth.

Let me ask you a couple of probing questions. Think before answering. If God were still writing His Word today, would you be in a chapter like this one? And if you were included, what would it say of you? I realize such a question could foster guilt. I don't mean it as such. My underlying desire is to challenge you toward greatness . . . to ask you to go far beyond the "adequate" . . . to refuse to settle for mediocrity.

A CHALLENGE TOWARD GREATNESS

Our sixteenth president often found relief and release by slipping into the New York Avenue Presbyterian Church and listening to Dr. Gurley, the pastor. The Civil War was ripping his heart apart. During those desperate, dark years, Lincoln was often down and discouraged. He would come to church with the expectation of finding fresh hope and encouragement. The president came with an aide, and the two of them would listen from the pastor's study, which adjoined the sanctuary, so as not to disrupt things.

At one particular Wednesday-night service, after the minister finished preaching and the people began to leave, the presidential aide leaned over and asked, "What did you think of the sermon?"

Lincoln replied, "I thought it was well thought through, powerfully delivered, and very eloquent."

"Then you thought it was a great sermon?" the aide continued.

"No," said Lincoln, "it failed."

"Failed? Why did it fail?" queried the aide.

Lincoln responded, "Because the pastor did not ask of us something great."[17]

This little booklet may fail for other reasons, but it won't because I failed to ask something great of you, my friend. I am committed to asking something great of you, not something easily achieved or something naturally accomplished. I urge you to make a difference! I am asking something great of you who live in a competitive environment, who work in a company, perhaps where Christ is never mentioned except in profanity. I'm asking something great of you who are rearing a family in a neighborhood where everyone else, it seems, is marching to a different drumbeat. I'm asking something great of you who are preparing your minds in school for a career marked by integrity. Perhaps you are in a seminary. It may be that you are a busy mother of several small children. Regardless of your situation, I'm ask-

ing something great of you. I'm asking that
you lift your sights above the status quo.
Perhaps it's been a long time since someone
looked you in the eye and challenged you to
break with your old habits and take on a
new and aggressive plan to follow the Lord
with your whole heart.

When God spoke to Noah, He didn't
tell him to kick back, relax, and wait for rain.
He said, "Build an ark!" Noah began that
unusual project and stayed with it for a hun-
dred and twenty years. Can you imagine the
words of the neighbors, watching a boat that
big being built, even though there had never
been rain? God asked a great thing of Noah.

When He spoke to Moses, He said,
"Lead an exodus!" Above those lonely howl-
ing winds of the Sinai wilderness, God
spoke strong words and got his attention. He
asked something great of Moses.

When God spoke to Joseph, He said, in
effect, "Forgive your brothers." It would
have been the easiest thing in the world for
Joseph to do what came naturally . . . to
retaliate, to get even, to pay them back.
Remember the scene? Years after ripping off
Joseph, his brothers walked up to him and
asked for a handout. Remember, Joseph
practically "owned" Egypt. All he had to do
was snap his fingers and those brothers
would have been history. Instead, he forgave
every one of them immediately and com-

pletely. God asked something great of Joseph.

How about young David? When God tapped David on the shoulder, He said, "Kill the giant." I'd call that a fairly great command!

When He spoke to the prophet Isaiah, He asked, "Who will go? Whom shall I send?" Isaiah's answer? After he was cleansed to be a spokesman for His Lord, Isaiah responded: "Here am I. Send me." God's plan completely changed the prophet's life.

When He talked to Peter, He said, "Feed My sheep." He didn't tell him to lick his wounds over his failures. He didn't condemn him for his past. He said, "Feed My sheep. Feed My lambs." God asked a great thing of Peter.

When He spoke to the old Pharisee, now turned Apostle of Grace, He said to him, "Come over to Macedonia and help us." He asked something great of Paul. And as a result, our European forefathers heard of Christ.

So, in this booklet, I do not hesitate to ask of you something great. The years ahead will become increasingly more difficult. Count on it. The church will deal with issues in the future that no one would have imagined fifty years ago. Seminaries must address things that were either never mentioned or that stayed on the back burner fifty years ago. Now they are front-burner stuff. Every media ministry will have its mettle tested. We face tests and temptations as never before. Our plate of changes is full and running over. Count on it. These are not easy times. These are hard times . . . harsh times. That is precisely the setting needed for the cultivation of character. I remind you yet again, this is no time for wimps!

It is enough to drive everyone of us back to our calling (which isn't a bad idea) and as we kneel before our Lord, tell Him, "I am willing to be wholeheartedly Yours. You live in my life, and it's time that I stop hiding it. It's time for me to come out of the closet and openly speak of You, the One who has saved me!"

While feeling a little sorry for myself recently, I found encouragement in the words of Oswald Chambers:

> If you are devoted to the cause of humanity, you will soon be exhausted and have your heart broken by ingratitude, but if the mainspring of your service is love for Jesus, you can serve men although they treat you as a doormat. Never look for justice in this world, but never cease to give it.[18]

MOSES: FRONT AND CENTER

So then, what is it, I ask? What specifically is this "great thing"? It's tucked away in the mini-biography of Moses, Hebrews 11:23–27. Remember his story?

> By faith Moses, when he was born, was hid for three months by his parents, because they saw that the child was beautiful. (v. 23)

His parents saw something in him from the beginning that was different. They sensed that God's hand was on their son, and that was worth special attention, so they protected and trained him early in his life. When he came of age, he "refused to be called the son of Pharaoh's daughter." You know why he had such courage? He learned it from his mother and father! Go back and look at the end of verse 23: ". . . and they were not afraid of the king's edict."

Isn't that great?

Years ago, while Lorne Sanny was president of The Navigators, he celebrated his sixtieth birthday. I asked him, "What's it like being sixty years old?" He had a great answer. "I'm not afraid of anybody."

I've always appreciated that answer. Now, don't misread what he said. We are to have a fear of God until the last breath we breathe on this earth, while at the same we have no reason to be afraid of others. What a healthy balance! That describes Moses' parents . . . and ultimately, Moses himself.

Isn't it strange how wimpy so many folks have become? We are surrounded by human beings who have us frightened. We live as though we serve a God who is impotent. We have the tables turned. It's time we came back to basics. Let's learn from Moses and from his parents. Let's stop being afraid of any human authority!

So when Moses was called the son of Pharaoh's daughter, he chose "rather to endure ill-treatment with the people of God, than to enjoy the passing pleasures of sin." Verse 27 says: ". . . he left Egypt, not fearing the wrath of the king."

What characterized his parents' life characterized his own. So we should not be at all surprised to read that he "endured." Don't you love that word? He remained "steadfast, immovable, abounding" in the work of his Lord.

- *The Living Bible* says, "He kept right on going."
- *The New International Version*, "He persevered."
- *The New English Bible*, "He was resolute."
- *The Amplified Bible* says, "He held staunchly to his purpose."
- *The Moffatt Bible*'s quaint rendering, "He never flinched."

  I love that about Moses!

Have you forgotten how old Moses was? Eighty! At that age when most of his peers would have been urging him to take it easy and relax, God said, "Take the shoes off your feet. You're standing on holy ground." He took off his sandals . . . stood there barefoot on the hot sands of the desert, and listened to this bush that wouldn't stop burning and wouldn't stop talking! The last voice he ever thought he would hear at that age was the voice of his God. I remind you, the voice did not say, "Relax, Moses. Next time you're back with your father-in-law, build a hammock. Hang out, man. Drink a little Sinai lemonade. Take it easy!" Not on your life. He told His eighty-year-old servant to return to Egypt and lead an exodus.

My physician in California told me a true story several years ago; it was an experience that resulted in something he learned the hard way. He was treating a lady who was in her eighties. She was in great physical and emotional condition.

He asked, "What in the world do you do to stay in such great condition?"

She answered, "Why, I run."

"You run?" he asked. "How far do you run?"

"Well, usually four or five miles," she responded.

With amazement he asked, "Every month?"

"Of course not . . . every day," she stated.

He said, "Oh, my! You'd better take it easy."

To his surprise, she took his advice . . . and in three months she was dead.

Now, she may have passed on for other reasons, but the point is, my physician said that he would never again tell a patient to "take it easy." He told me that he had taken those words out of his vocabulary.

A PLEA FOR ENDURANCE

My message to you today, especially you who are tempted to back off and leave this mess we're in for someone else to handle: Endure! Don't take it easy. Step up to the plate. Pay attention to life and determine what you are going to contribute. Who knows but what you were brought onto this earth for this very moment. It may be that your best investment will be in your children's lives. You may have grandchildren who are in the middle of their growing-up years. Don't take it easy with the grandkids! Pour your life into them! Pass on the things you have learned . . . and don't omit mentioning the hardships and the heartaches of your own life. Spend time with those who will take the torch to the next generation and march our country into the twenty-first century. Don't take it easy.

I especially fear for you in midlife, when it is so easy to sell yourself to a comfortable lifestyle. Being middle-aged is a treacherous time.

C. S. Lewis once wrote of those "long, dull, monotonous years of middle-aged prosperity or middle-aged adversity," which he called, "excellent campaigning weather for the devil."[19]

You may have become so busy making a living that you've forgotten about making a life. You may be so busy with your financial portfolio that you've forgotten the importance of personal character. It is that, my friend, which can most effectively impact our own generation that has lost its way. Our young are looking for those who are determined; still teachable; flexible, yet firm in convictions; those who can handle the obstacles and endure whatever may be thrown at them.

Several days ago one of the people on our staff at Dallas Seminary dropped by my office for a brief visit. Before leaving he handed me a small framed picture. It was an overhead view of a skier. This skier was going full-speed ahead downhill, through moguls and down steep slopes. They looked enormous, even from the air. All the way down he was kicking up massive sprays of snow. A simple quotation appeared at the bottom of the picture that put everything into perspective: "Obstacles are those frightful things you see when you take your mind off the goals." I would suggest you memorize that statement!

It is possible that you have become obstacle-conscious. All you know is the bad news. Your focus is on what isn't working. You're one of the best prophets of doom this generation has produced! You know what won't work. You're notorious for your complaining and whining. Furthermore, you're hard to live with. Time out! Why not break with that negativistic, pessimistic mentality. We need strong-hearted men and women today who refuse to let obstacles deter them.

Thomas Carlyle, the Scottish essayist, said, "The block of granite which stands as an obstacle in the pathway of the weak becomes a stepping stone in the pathway of the strong." Carlyle is correct! Those obstacles are planned by our Father, who, rather than blocking our way, is working on building our character. So, endure!

Moses endured during his eighties, his nineties, and on far past his one-hundredth birthday. He endured despite the contempt of Pharaoh. He endured in spite of the stubbornness of the Hebrews, who grumbled and maligned and complained and rebelled. He endured despite the criticism of those closest to him—Aaron, Miriam, Dathan, Abiram. He endured despite being disappointed at the spies who returned more impressed with the odds against them than with the God who was for them. He endured! The question is: How?

The text tells us. He endured because he kept his eyes fixed. . . . "He endured, as seeing him who is invisible" (Heb. 11:27). He didn't lose sight of the goal. He knew there was an ultimate plan, and that the people of God would get to the land God had promised. Moses realized he would be the human conduit on this earth who would enable them to get there.

On the basis of Moses' example, I challenge you to endure, to stand firm, to be steadfast, to model faithfulness.

Periodically, I have attended a professional baseball game between two excellent teams. I find games like that very interesting. Here comes a top-notch batter to the plate, ready to face a terrific pitcher. Both are great ball players. The batter walks up as the pitcher glares at him. After a few scratches, spits, swings in the air, and settling in, the batter gets that bat ready. He acts absolutely unintimidated, as if to say to the pitcher, "You do your worst; I will do my best." Soon, the ball comes flying over ninety miles an hour and—crack! The hitter slams that ball out of that park. Incredible! What a lesson to learn from such champion athletes. It's tough at that plate . . . incredible pressure, requiring relentless determination . . . but there they stand and do their best.

Endure, my friend, even when conspirators seem to prosper. Even when critics won't shut up. Even when the wicked seem to be winning. Even when the pressure seems unbearable. Stand fast! Even when big people act contemptibly small. Even when you feel as though you're all alone, even when "truth is on the scaffold and wrong is on the throne." Stay strong. Endure, regardless!

I return often to the words of Churchill, "I have not become the king's First Minister in order to preside over the liquidation of the British Empire."[20] God brings certain people on earth to face stern challenges. To make it very personal, I was not led to begin Insight for Living so that I might witness its demise. I was not brought to Dallas Theological Seminary to pronounce a quiet eulogy. I was brought to these ministries to give them the kind of leadership it takes to endure. And by His grace we will become stronger and stronger. We are not kicking back. God's hand is on His work, and the gates of hell will not prevail against it. It will not fail. It is not in vain. Nor is your life. Nor is His plan for your life. You, too, have been prepared for God's purposes in your life. I challenge you to meet them head-on.

THREE PROMISES FOR YOU TO CLAIM

What can I promise you? Three specific things. First, *on this earth* I can promise you (to borrow from Churchill) "blood, toil, tears, and sweat." Quite possibly, the hardest times you've ever experienced are before you, not behind you. Second, if you determine to live as I've been writing about, I can promise that *on your gravestone* will appear the words (to borrow from Paul), "not in vain." Your life will not have been lived in vain. Third, *on your crown*, I can promise you these words (to borrow from Jesus): "Well done, good and faithful servant. Enter into the joy of the Lord." Then—and only then—you will hear, "Kick back. Take it easy. The job's done."

May our Lord give you the best days of your life as you gear up for what's ahead. If you need to make a change in order for that to happen, what are you waiting for? As our nation was fifty years ago, we are now in a struggle for survival. Hard times call for people fully committed to Jesus Christ, who are not afraid of being different in order to make a difference. Will you be one of them? Good for you! I stand with you. Times like these require such a commitment . . . nothing more, nothing less, nothing else.

This is no time for wimps!

NOTES

1   William Manchester, *The Last Lion, Winston Spencer Churchill* (Boston, Mass.: Little, Brown & Company, 1983), 4.

2   Sir Winston Churchill, as quoted by John Bartlett in *Familiar Quotations*, 15th ed., revised and enlarged, ed. Emily Morison Beck (Boston: Little, Brown & Company, 1980), 743.

3   Sir Winston Churchill, as quoted by William Manchester, *The Last Lion, Winston Spencer Churchill*, 6.

4   Sir Winston Churchill, *Great War Speeches*, Comp. Charles Eade (London: Transworld Publishers, Corgi Books, 1965), 128.

5   Churchill, *Great War Speeches*, 129.

6   Churchill, *Familiar Quotations*, 74.

7   Churchill, *Familiar Quotations*, 745.

8   Churchill, *Familiar Quotations*, 746.

9   Churchill, *Great War Speeches*, 128.

10 James Russell Lowell, as quoted in *Illustrations Unlimited*, ed. James S. Hewett (Wheaton, Ill.: Tyndale, 1988), 59.

11 James Russell Lowell, *Familiar Quotations*, 567.

12 John Henry Jowett, as quoted by Warren W. Wiersbe and David Wiersbe in *Making Sense of the Ministry* (Grand Rapids: Baker, 1983, 1989), 36.

13 Dwight L. Moody, as quoted in *Great Quotes & Illustrations*, compiled by George Sweeting (Waco, Tex.: Word Books, 1985), 43.

14 Johann Goethe, *Familiar Quotations*, 395.

15 Thomas Paine, *Familiar Quotations*, 384.

16 Aleksandr I. Solzhenitsyn, *The Gulag Archipelago* (New York: Harper & Row, 1973), as quoted by Philip Yancey in *Where Is God When It Hurts?* (Grand Rapids: Zondervan, 1977), 51.

17 Adapted from Bruce Larson's, *What God Wants to Know* (San Francisco: Harper San Francisco, 1993), 46–47.

18 Oswald Chambers, *Oswald Chambers: The Best from All*

His Books, comp. and ed. Harry Verploegh (Nashville: Nelson, 1987), 320.

19 C. S. Lewis, *The Screwtape Letters*, revised edition (New York: Collier Books, Macmillan, 1982), 132.

20 Sir Winston Churchill, *Familiar Quotations*, 746.